clos

CW00538872

my poetry journal

valeria abelli

Advanced Praise for CLOSURE

"*Closure* offers a raw, unmolded journey through a healing process. Abelli takes a brave swing by leaving a journal of heartbreak on the table, open-handed."

— Lorenz Alexander, Author of *All One*

"Abelli pulls at your healing heartstrings in this diary of love and heartbreak. It resonates deeply and leaves one feeling less alone in the messiness that can be love felt, love lost and love gained."

— Flor Ana, Author of *The Truth About Love*

"Valeria Abelli's *Closure* is the roadmap we all need when in the midst of healing from profound heartbreak. With candid intimacy, Abelli takes readers behind the curtain of genuine healing, empowering them to reclaim their own closure. Abelli captures the non-linear, sometimes messy, path of healing from wounds not visible to the naked eye."

— Elizabeth Knightly, Author of *Choose To Choose Me*

"*Closure* is a beautiful and relatable unraveling of the feelings and thoughts of heartbreak. Abelli has a perfect execution of what it feels like to bleed love while fighting one's own brain until there is finally closure."

— Kendall Hope, Author of *The Willow Weepings*

"Abelli's poetry reads like a song, and it is as though each of these poems encompasses every art form imaginable. This stunning collection of poetry is how art and poetry exist in conversation with each other, and the use of the timestamps at the beginning of each poem grounds the reader and carries them along through the storyline and evolution of this collection."

— Kristen Richards, Author of *The Desert is a Woman Too*

Continued Advanced Praise for CLOSURE

"*Closure* is a confessional diary, dripping with vulnerability and contradiction. It's an honest look into the mapless path to healing from heartbreak. Paired illustrations unfold layers of imagery in her poetic entries, each informing the other like windows into her subconscious. Abelli holds nothing back."

— Katie Scruggs Galloway, Author of *Still and Still Moving*

"Through a timeline of journal entries and illustrations, Abelli takes the reader through a personal journey of hurt and healing. The vulnerability and raw poetry showcase how heartbreak can be transcended and how we can carry on as a clock strikes a new hour. "

— Fin Rose Aborizk, Author of *On The Ever-Lovely Morrow*

Copyright © 2024 by Valeria Abelli

All rights reserved.

This book (or any portion thereof) may not be reproduced or used in any manner without written permission from the author except in the context of reviews.

Cover Art Copyright © 2024 by Valentina Delgado
Illustrations Copyright © 2024 by Valentina Delgado

Edited by Flor Ana Mireles

1st Edition | 01
Paperback ISBN: 979-8-9895551-5-4

First Published May 2024

For inquiries and bulk orders, please email:
indieearthpublishinghouse@gmail.com

Printed in the United States of America 1 2 3 4 5 6 7 8 9

Indie Earth Publishing Inc.
| Miami, FL |

www.indieearthbooks.com

this is me closing the door to our past

"Closure" is dedicated to anyone who's in the process of healing from heartbreak. It is okay to rant about a situation as many times as you need to. It is okay to go out and have fun one night and then spend the next day crying, regretting your drunk decisions from the night before. It is okay to go back and put yourself in a situation over and over again until you feel strong enough to leave it. There is no handbook that explains the perfect way to heal because it doesn't exist.

This collection of poetry shows a realistic healing journey. It is never linear and the dates and timestamps on these poems prove that. These poems were taken straight from my diary. As an artist, my songwriting process usually starts from poems or rants I have written. I decided to let you guys in from a different perspective, through poetry.

I appreciate writing in all aspects and, to me, songwriting and poetry go hand in hand. I hold this work close to my heart because it is the most vulnerable I have allowed myself to get with what I've put out so far. Writing this book helped me heal from situations I hadn't taken the time to deal with yet. Face your emotions and work on yourself. Don't give someone else the power to give you closure.

JULY 13, 2022 02:15

my body is tarnished from your touch.
your remnants stained my heart,
yearning to go back to the start
when your beautiful lies made me blush.

~ *can we start over?*

JULY 16, 2022 13:56

did you know this was gonna go down
when i got on that plane to milan?
was this part of your master plan?
was that kiss where the end began?

JULY 25, 2022 23:39

you said you'd never hurt me
and i said i'd never leave.

~ *i guess we both lied*

JULY 29, 2022 13:14

i miss my sweet boy.

~ *change*

JULY 31, 2022 16:45

i was the girl who never stopped laughing
and you took that away from me.

AUGUST 8, 2022 16:04

i had you on a pedestal
and you stomped on me.
i always felt so small.
you kept standing tall.
you're still 6'2 &
i'm still not over you.

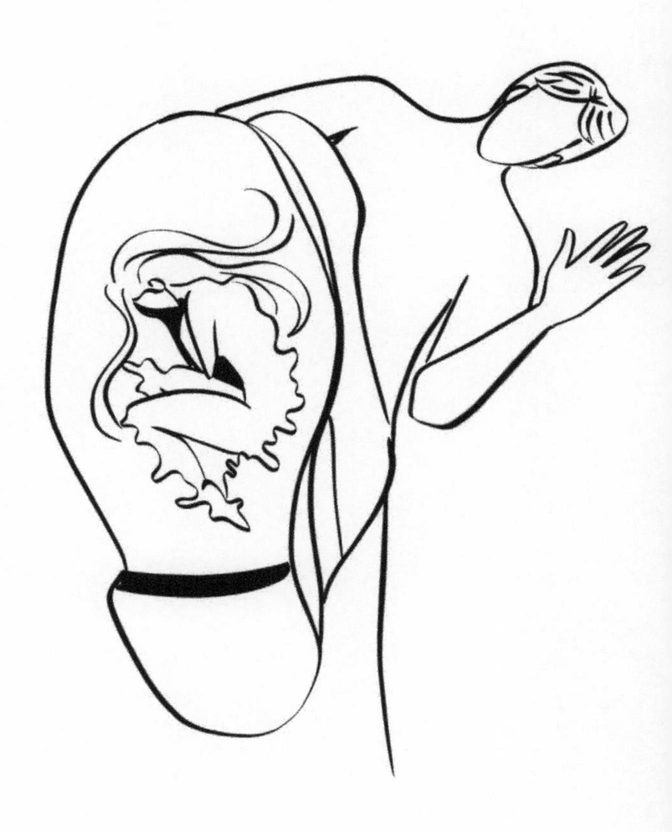

AUGUST 19, 2022 17:52

you said the uber canceled that night and stayed till 6 am...
it was all a lie.

~ *master manipulator*

SEPTEMBER 5, 2022 15:32

i could never get out the words in time before you threw the knife.
your poisoned words made a hole in my heart simply out of spite.

~ i'm still bleeding

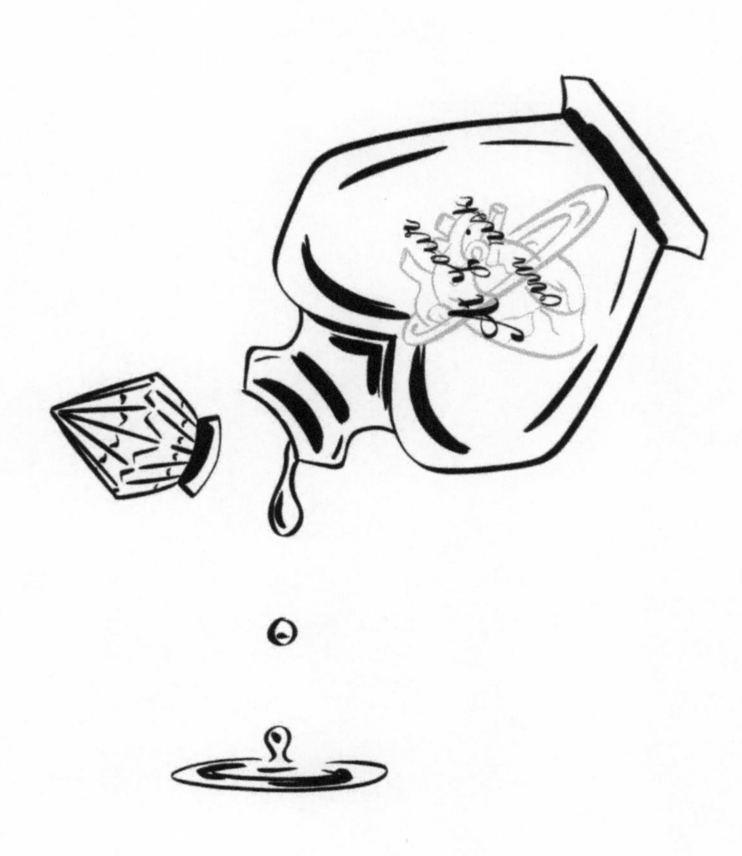

SEPTEMBER 15, 2022 3:09

i don't know who i am without you
but i do know i'm better off
and that says so much.

SEPTEMBER 18, 2022 22:21

you learned things about me
no one else cared enough
to know of.

SEPTEMBER 23, 2022 18:17

no one knows what we went through
when we were together
except me and you,
but everyone knows what i went through
when we finally ended
except you.

~ irony

SEPTEMBER 27, 2022 22:13

i didn't leave 'cause i didn't love you.
i had to go because i was forced to.
i would've stayed and fixed it;
i didn't need any convincing.

OCTOBER 10, 2022 22:35

my friends hate you and i defend you.
i don't have dignity left to lose.
you
make
me
look
stupid.

OCTOBER 18, 2022 18:09

your heart has claw marks.

~ i still can't let go

OCTOBER 28, 2022 00:19

i was wired to look for you in every guy
from the moment i was forced to say goodbye.

~ why couldn't you just try?

OCTOBER 31, 2022 02:05

attachment is scary; you were a haunted house.

NOVEMBER 6, 2022 02:57

you came back, 2:54 am.
your brother begged me to stay.
you had three minutes.
in 180 seconds, i forgave,
i forgot about the past
and we fell back to the start.

~ i'm gonna regret this

DECEMBER 27, 2022 05:00

i say i don't regret you
when it's 2 am on a friday night and the vodka made me forget it all.
i say i don't regret you
when it's 4 am on a saturday night and the weed made you want to call.
i say i don't regret you
'cause you cried to me that night in your car.
i say i don't regret you
'cause i don't want to be seen as discarded.
but when it's 3 pm on sunday and the memories start to come back,
i regret it all and the hangover shivers become triggering flashbacks.
at the expense of my heart, you got what you wanted.
on november 6, i shouldn't have responded.

~ *i do regret you*

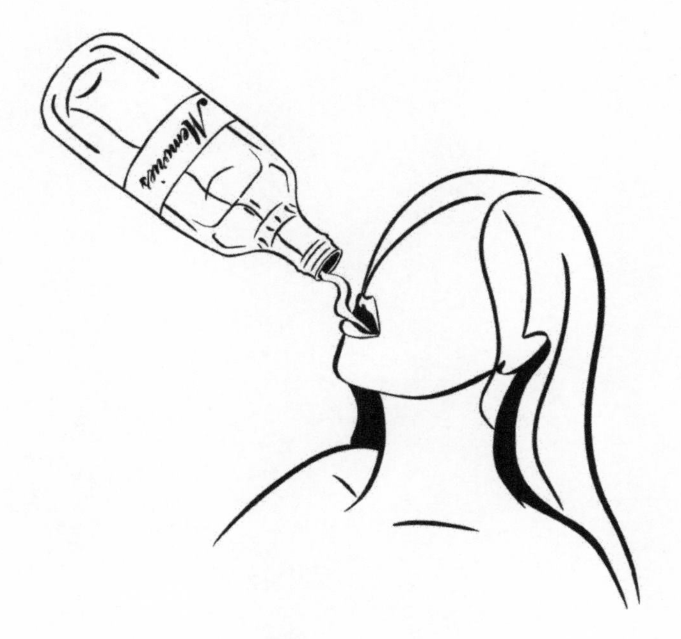

DECEMBER 30, 2022 22:49

i confessed to you every single insecurity
and in the end you used them all against me.

~ how do you sleep at night?

DECEMBER 31, 2022 23:12

you can complain all you want,
but i promise no one will ever love you like i did.

~ how could you do this again?

JANUARY 1, 2023 00:02

you know me better than anyone.
i don't think i ever knew you at all.

~ you're staying in 2022

CLOSURE

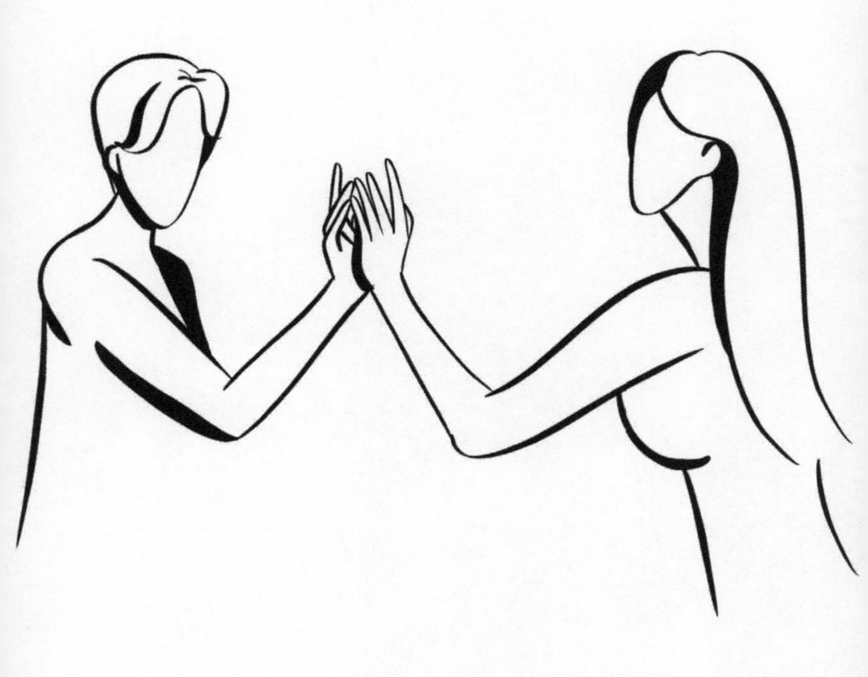

JANUARY 3, 2023 03:04

at what point did you stop caring?
at what point does it stop hurting?

~ *dangerous curiosity*

JANUARY 14, 2023 16:22

you always said “right person, wrong time,”
but you just didn’t know how to treat me right.

JANUARY 15, 2023 23:08

you're the only birthday text i'm waiting for.

~ *delusion*

JANUARY 23, 2023 03:24

i'm not crazy, i was there.
you DID fucking care.

~ internal battle

JANUARY 25, 2023 22:09

it's funny how quickly things change.
from stranger to friends
in one conversation.
you became my best friend.

everything was right,
nothing could possibly go wrong.
it was only up from here.

it's funny how quickly things change.
from friends to lovers
in a heartbeat.
you made the rain go away.
the skies turned blue,
the grass was greener,
my heart beat faster,
butterflies lived in my stomach.

everything was right,
nothing could possibly go wrong.
except... it was only down from here.

it's funny how quickly things change.
from lovers to strangers
in just one fight.
it was pouring tears.
the skies turned gray,
the grass was dirt,
my heart beat faster,
anxiety lived in my stomach.

everything went wrong,
nothing ended right.
it was rock bottom.

- but it's only up from here

JANUARY 28, 2023 15:34

i had to go back to you a million times to finally hate you.

~ the hatred was love in disguise

JANUARY 29, 2023 02:15

you made me feel like a side character in my own story.

~ i lost all control

FEBRUARY 5, 2023 23:47

i shouldn't have let you see that part of me.

~ you weren't worthy

FEBRUARY 14, 2023 21:03

you convinced me i was fucking crazy.
i made you believe you were amazing.
it was never equal.

FEBRUARY 18, 2023 15:37

no book or song is enough to write about all the ways you fucked me up, but it's worth the effort.

MARCH 5, 2023 22:10

i saw you today, because i knew where to find you.
same place, same time; i'll take the blame.
i acted like i didn't see you, and you did too.
you believed i was okay and i believed you were unphased.
your heart remains stoic while mine remains devoted.

~ it was a coincidence, i swear

MARCH 6, 2023 23:15

your friends saw me.
did they tell you?
do you talk about me?

i miss you, you know that?

i saw your friends.
i'm dying to tell you.
did they talk about me?

i hate them, you know that.

~ *bad influence*

MARCH 8, 2023 15:45

text me.
call me.
come see me.
get drunk and do it.
i promise i'll answer.
please.

MARCH 9, 2023 23:30

you broke me, but
i'll pick up the pieces
of my shattered heart
you once kept whole
and i'll be okay.
you'll come back
when it's too late.
you might be my weakness,
but even i have a limit.

~ *for cata*

MARCH 10, 2023 00:28

the gym is packed, yet all i see is your silhouette.
running 100 miles an hour won't make me forget.
am i supposed to pretend everything is okay?
am i supposed to pretend i didn't beg you to stay?

"everything happens for a reason" is
forever engraved in my arm now.
a broken heart was all it took
to change the body you once knew.

it's obvious my anxiety is peaking through,
but your deadly stare doesn't take the clue.
am i supposed to pretend i don't know you?
are you pretending not to see my tattoo?

"everything happens for a reason."
we were supposed to get it together,
but a broken heart was all i needed
to change the girl who was mistreated.

the gym is packed, yet all i see is your silhouette.
my heart is beating out of my chest; you won't break a sweat.
how do you pretend everything is okay?
how do you pretend you didn't want me to stay?

i can tell it hurts to see my tattoo.
no one knows you like i do.
"everything happens for a reason..."
one day i'll know that reason.

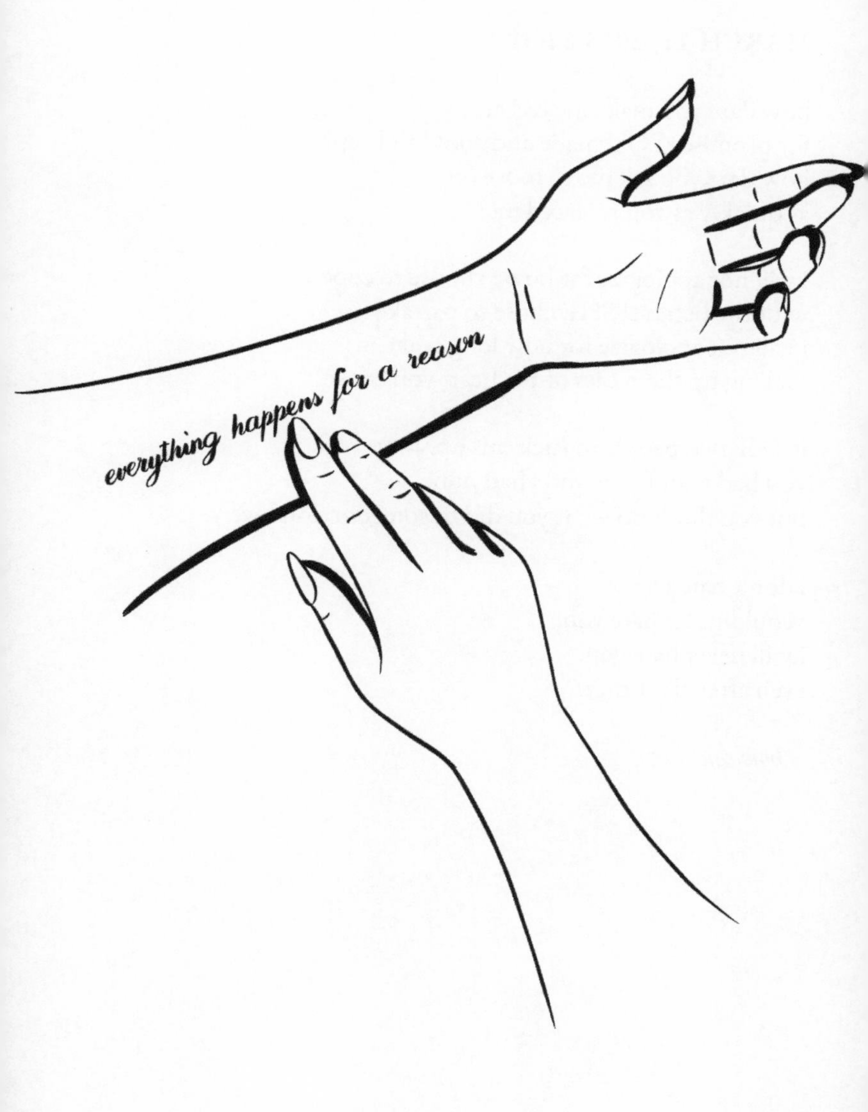
everything happens for a reason

MARCH 11, 2023 22:31

how dare you make me feel crazy
for promises YOU made and couldn't keep?
how dare you ask me to move on
as quickly as you replaced me?

i will not apologize for how i choose to cope
with the betrayal SHE chose to partake in.
i will not apologize for how long i take in
picking up the pieces of the heart you broke.

it took two people to fuck this up.
you had your faults and i had mine,
but you don't do what you did to someone you love.

i don't hate you.
i could never hate you.
i will never hate you,
even after all of that.

~ *how could i?*

MARCH 12, 2023 22:57

from the bottom of my heart,
fuck you for coming back.

~ respectfully, of course.

MARCH 17, 2023 16:04

you stopped caring
and i stopped eating.
you started calling
and i started drinking.

~ coping

MARCH 26, 2023 02:06
a stranger really knows this girl.
he loved everything about her,
so he kissed every inch of her body
and took the innocence she held dearly.

this stranger confides in her.
only she has seen him cry,
only she has touched him.
he's truly himself with her.

a stranger really knows this guy.
she loved him more than life,
so she gave him the innocence she held dearly
and he broke her trust and scarred her body.

this stranger is attached to him.
only he has seen her cry,
only he has touched her,
but she lost herself with him.

two strangers who couldn't love each other right,
a potential relationship they had to leave behind.
two strangers who have tried and tried and tried,
but the consequential disaster still fucks with her mind.

two strangers who have seen each other at their worst,
a potential relationship that has always been cursed.
she brought out the best in him and he knew that;
he has power over her and he loves that.

two strangers who won't let each other go
and probably never really will.

~ *unspoken truths*

MARCH 29, 2023 19:13

i lost friends because of the way you changed me;
i could even stand myself anymore.

MARCH 30, 2023 02:17

it's hard to fall asleep when your last words still terrorize me.
they cut deep.

APRIL 15, 2023 23:45

why do you keep calling?
i'll pretend i don't know who it is and you'll pretend it was an accident.

~ *we're lying to ourselves*

APRIL 29, 2023 22:14

it's hard to end the chapter when i lose track and keep starting over.
you don't let me heal.
stop calling me.

MAY 7, 2023 18:58

people ask me what it is about you
and i never have an answer.

you ran two blocks under the rain
to see me when i wasn't okay.
you complimented my brain
and cared about what i had to say.

i don't think i'm crazy for falling for you,
but insane to believe you had fallen too.

you did everything just right enough,
then left me hanging when things got tough.

~ i still don't have an answer

MAY 10, 2023 17:56

i'll always have a soft spot for you.

MAY 16, 2023 21:23

you told so many lies
i started questioning myself.

~ gaslighting

MAY 18, 2023 23:17

i couldn't go to sleep if i didn't see your mind wasn't at ease.
how do you sleep at night knowing i have the scars from your knife?

~ it's not fair, it never has been

JUNE 3, 2023 03:15

do you ever regret losing me?

JUNE 17, 2023 23:19

i won't lie and say it hasn't been hard
'cause my heart still drops when i see a red car.

~ *where were you going?*

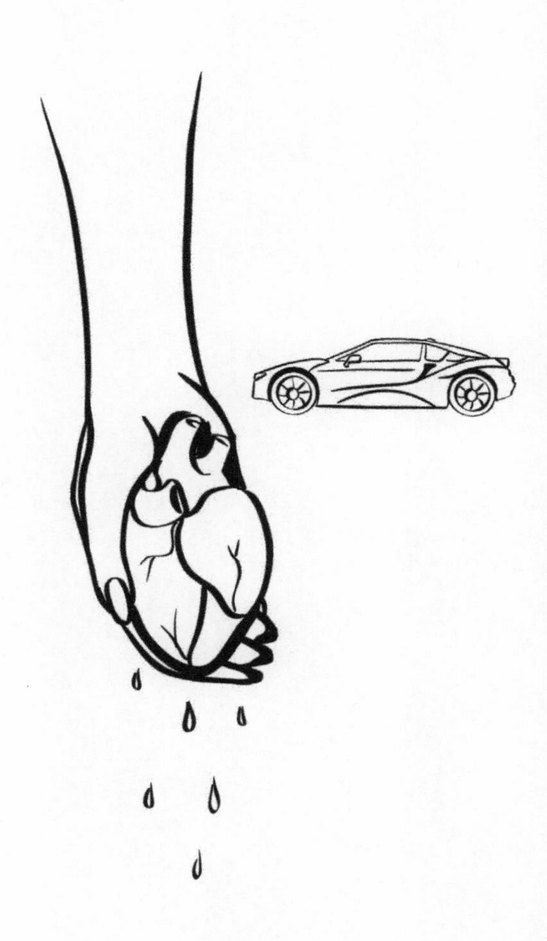

JUNE 20, 2023 14:45

it WAS tragic.
i wasn't dramatic.

JUNE 28, 2023 18:16

i wish you the best.

~ *karma*

JULY 1, 2023 00:59

the. cycle. ends. now.

~ *i forgive myself*

JULY 4, 2023 22:16

i'll never love anyone the way i loved you,
but someone will love me the way you never could.

~ *hopeless romantic*

JULY 13, 2023 17:23

so many songs you'll never listen to,
so many poems you'll never read.
wait—
i lied.

~ *my voice*

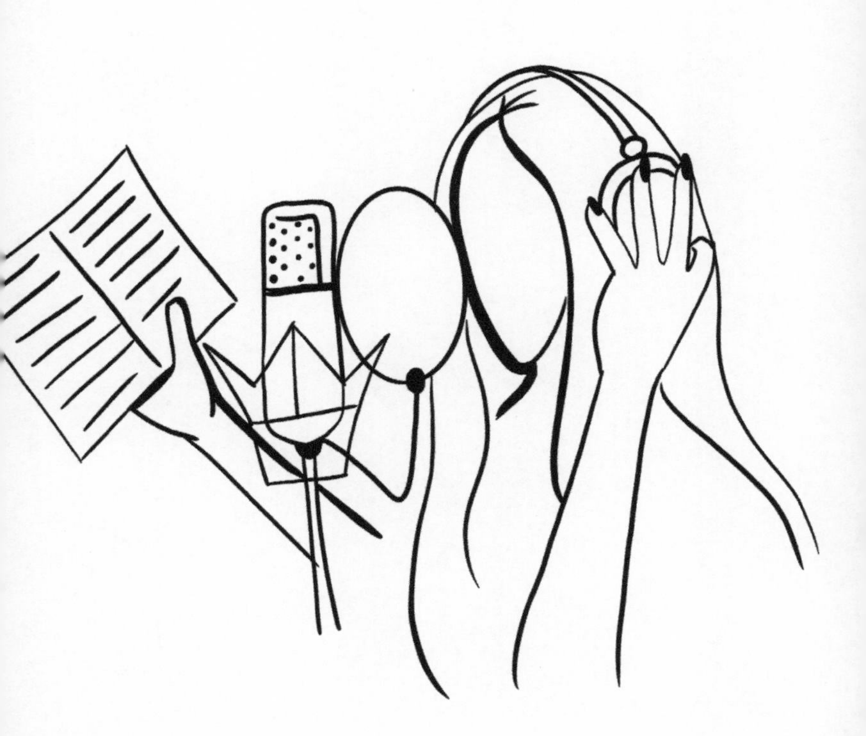

JULY 19, 2023 23:29

you judged my brutal reactions.
i justified your cruel actions.
we are NOT the same.

JULY 26, 2023 22:45

i can't recognize who i used to be.
you destroyed me.

AUGUST 15, 2023 16:04

i blamed your friends for the person you became,
but time revealed *everything* was your fault.

AUGUST 16, 2023 22:16

your brother hates me 'cause of you... (2022)
i love him like a brother too... (2023)

she'll take your side, i'm sure of that... (2022)
your cousin is the sister i never had... (2023)

i hate him; he's the reason you changed... (2022)
i love him; he's the reason i'm okay... (2023)

~ *plot twist*

SEPTEMBER 23, 2023 23:56

you complain about my writing,
but i think you secretly enjoy it.

~ *narcissism*

OCTOBER 27, 2023 01:13

you will always be the villain in my story.

JANUARY 5, 2024 02:51

i miss you as a friend sometimes,
but then again, how could i ever be your friend?

JANUARY 24, 2024 11:04

i don't think i ever really got over what you put me through,
but i know the end of it was the start of what you turned into
and i hope that haunts you.

JANUARY 29, 2024 13:15

the only peace of mind i have is
i know the truth will come out with time.

~ songwriting

FEBRUARY 17, 2024 23:56

you don't have power over me anymore.

~ closure

acknowledgments

A special thanks to Adrian Nucete, Andres Rodriguez, Catalina Prieto, Diego Castellanos, Fabiana Rojas, Gabriela Fuentes, José Linares, Nina Encarnación, and Santiago Alvarez for being the people who stuck by my side through everything and inspired me to see the positive in the disaster that was my life at the time. A heartfelt thanks to my older brother Angelo and his wife Cristina for always having my back, my little brother Alessandro for his support, and most of all my parents, Cesar And Patrizia, who have been my biggest cheerleaders in everything I do and continue to encourage me to put my best work out there. With much love, I thank Enzo Di Giovanni, my amazing boyfriend, who has been incredible in this whole process and has pushed me to continue to write about my stories through music and poetry. His unconditional love and support has powered me through the harder moments and helped me get stronger. Thank you to Valentina Delgado for using her artistic talents to bring my work to life with her drawings. Lastly, I am so grateful for my amazing editor, Flor Ana Mireles, and publisher, Indie Earth, for leading me on this journey and helping me every step of the way.

about the author

VALERIA ABELLI is a singer/songwriter born and raised in Miami, Florida to Venezuelan parents. She has been playing instruments since she was a little girl. Most of her songs are derived from her diary and is currently graduating from Berklee College of Music with a B.A. in Songwriting and will continue pursuing her music career parallel to becoming an author. Her debut poetry collection "*Closure*" is only the beginning of her journey.

Connect with Valeria on Instagram:
@valeriaabelli

about the publisher

Indie Earth Publishing is an author-first, independent co-publishing company based in Miami, FL. A publisher for writers by a writer, Indie Earth offers the support and technical assistance of traditional publishing without asking writers and authors to compromise on their creative freedom. Each Indie Earth Author is part of an inspired and creative community, making a difference one book at a time.
For more titles from Indie Earth, or to inquire about publication, please visit:

www.indieearthbooks.com

For inquiries, please email:
indieearthpublishinghouse@gmail.com

Instagram: @indieearthbooks

Milton Keynes UK
Ingram Content Group UK Ltd.
UKHW012308060524
442290UK00004B/233

9 798989 555154